About this book

Many children have difficulty puzzling out letters because they are abstract symbols. Letterland's worldwide success is all about its enduring characters who give these symbols life and stop them from being abstract. In this book we meet Eddie the Elephant, Fireman Fred and Golden Girl. Their story is carefully designed to emphasise the sounds that the letters 'E', 'F' and 'G' make in words. This definitive, original story book is an instant collector's classic, making learning fun for a new generation of readers.

A TEMPLAR BOOK

This edition published in the UK in 2008 by Templar Publishing
an imprint of The Templar Company plc,
The Granary, North Street, Dorking, Surrey, RH4 1DN, UK
www.templarco.co.uk

First published by Hamlyn Publishing, 1985
Devised and produced by The Templar Company plc

ISBN 978-1-84011-775-2

Printed in China

Letterland © was devised by and is the copyright of Lyn Wendon
LETTERLAND® is a registered trademark

Classic *LETTERLAND*
Storybooks

Eddy Elephant
and the Forest Fire

Also featuring
Fireman Fred and Golden Girl

Written by Lyn Wendon

Illustrated by
Jane Launchbury

templar publishing

Eddy Elephant was walking beside the lake with an empty expression on his face. He was making a big effort to think.

He wanted to make a float for the Flower Festival, but he could not think of an exciting idea.

"Hello Eddy!" called Fireman Fred who was fishing near by. "Have you finished your float yet? I have finished mine. It is my fire engine, completely covered with flowers!"

"That sounds excellent," said Eddy.

Suddenly Eddy's face brightened up. Fireman Fred had given him an idea.

"I'll have an engine, too," he said, "a different sort of engine. I think I can make one, but can you pull it for me?"

Fortunately, Fireman Fred said yes. So Eddy started to collect some logs to make his engine.

"Don't forget the Flower Festival parade starts at eleven o'clock at the Fire Station," called Fred.
"I won't forget," said Eddy Elephant.

Just then Golden Girl arrived.
She was in her Go-car.
"Hello, Fred," she called.

"I've come to gather some flowers.
I'm going to make my Go-car look
really gorgeous for the Flower Festival
tomorrow. Can you help me to pick
the flowers?"

Soon Fireman Fred and Golden Girl
had filled her Go-car with flowers.
There was no more time for fishing,
so Fireman Fred climbed into Golden
Girl's car and they both drove home.

"Don't forget to be at the Fire Station
at eleven," said Fireman Fred again.
"I won't forget," said Golden Girl.

At eleven o'clock the next day, Eddy Elephant rolled up to the Fire Station.

Everyone was delighted to see his float. It looked like an Express Train. It was painted red and black and on the side it said,

ELEPHANT EXPRESS.

Eddy sat on top wearing an engine driver's cap.

Fireman Fred and Fireman Frank had made their fire engine look almost like a forest of flowers!

Soon they were all ready to drive off to the parade, with Eddy's float in tow behind.

Then they heard Golden Girl racing up behind them. Her Go-car really did look gorgeous with golden rod flowers glued to the top and sides.

Golden Girl waved at them, but her face looked very grim.
"Stop, stop, stop!" she cried.
"Forget the parade. There's a fire in the forest! Follow me!"

"This sounds like an emergency!" exclaimed Eddy. The two firemen rushed to clear the flowers away from the fire hoses.

In a flash the fire engine was racing off towards the forest, with Eddy's Elephant Express close behind.

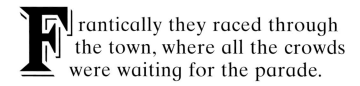**F**rantically they raced through the town, where all the crowds were waiting for the parade.

They passed Bouncy Ben's brass band.

They passed the grandstand where the prizes for the best float would be given out.

More flowers flew off the fire engine. Fireman Frank began to raise the ladder, ready to start fighting the fire.

When they reached the forest, the flames were already fifty feet high.

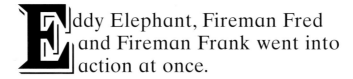

Eddy Elephant, Fireman Fred and Fireman Frank went into action at once.

Eddy Elephant sucked up a trunkful of water from the lake. Then he raced to the fire's edge and sprayed water everywhere.

Fireman Frank flooded the nearest flames with foam. Meanwhile, Fireman Frank rushed up the ladder with his hose and sprayed the highest flames.

Golden Girl grabbed some buckets and used her Go-car to carry more water up from the lake.

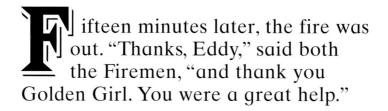

Fifteen minutes later, the fire was out. "Thanks, Eddy," said both the Firemen, "and thank you Golden Girl. You were a great help."

"It's lucky you saw the fire on your way to the parade," said Frank. "Otherwise the whole forest might have gone up in flames!"

"I suppose we are too late for the parade," said Eddy Elephant, looking sadly at the fire engine. Hardly any flowers were left on it.

Most of the flowers were gone from Golden Girl's Go-car as well.

"Never mind," said Frank. "Let's go and see who won the parade. We can still pull your Elephant Express."

So off they went. Eddy sat proudly on his Elephant Express, with the firemen in front and Golden Girl going on ahead.

As they came into the town they were very surprised to hear everyone cheering.

"Who are they cheering?"
asked Eddy.

Fireman Fred listened to the cheers and looked at everyone waving.
Then he smiled.

"I think they are cheering us," he said.

They were! Everyone had heard about the forest fire, and how Eddy and Golden Girl had helped the two firemen put it out.

When the four of them arrived in front of the grandstand, everyone cheered even more loudly.

There was the King with four enormous garlands of flowers.

"I'm sorry we missed the parade," said Eddy.

"Oh, but you didn't," said the King. "We watched you racing past on your way to the fire. These garlands are the prizes for the fastest fire-fighting floats in Letterland!"

THE END